GHOST FLOWERS

A POETIC REMEDY
FROM THE REBEL & MYSTIC HEART

ALI BADSHAH

GHOST
FLOWERS

Published by Les Maîtres Conteurs (Canada)

ISBN 978-1-9995620-3-8

1. Poetry   2. Love   3. Life   4. Inspiration   5. Growth
6. Loss   7. Grief   8. Death   9. Magic

CONTENTS

III. LIFE 83

ABOUT THE AUTHOR   163

FOREWORD

It's already been written – in the laughter of the babies, the bleached bones dotting the deserts, the tears running down our faces, and the hearts that beat to the collective rhythm.

Our words are just an attempt to capture the love, clarity, and inspiration that breathe in and around us.

Ghost Flowers is a collection of hard-won insights, gained along the path that chose me.

ACKNOWLEDGEMENTS

Beyond the Most High, praise and prayers for all the angels, prophets, pirs, gurus, sages, mystics, and spirits who have helped us to embrace the Truth within.

To my Baba – my teacher – Murat Coskun, of the Rifa`i Sufi Order and The Canadian Institute of Sufi Studies: It has been my greatest fortune, and salvation, to be your student. Your compassion, wisdom, humour, and understanding have made all this possible. You continue to be a living lesson in love, clarity, and inspiration for me. I am forever grateful. I love you.

To my Ammi – my mom: You have always nurtured my rebel and mystic heart. You saw a light in me and never gave up. You are the embodiment of positive reinforcement and my measure of the greatest parent. I love you.

To my children: You are my hearts, my tigers. Our time together has been the greatest joy in my life; our time apart has been my greatest point of despair and, ultimately, growth. The truth is that we are, have been, and always will be together. I love you.

To my path partners: We have always known each other. I love you.

To all the demons, both inside and outside of me: Thank you for the pain, anger, sorrow, and heartbreak that brought me here. I love you.

YOU

BREATHING SPACE

The space between
　the hurt and the healed
　　is a single breath.

SACRED SPOT

Your bludgeoned mind and bleeding heart,
Start to heal with time apart,
From desires unfulfilled and crafted expectations,
With fires that crackle, burning your sensations.

You see, the bliss that's been amiss,
Like your first love's kiss,
Has been living in the space,
Where egos have their trysts.

It's a sacred spot with no room for thoughts,
No room for schemes, no room for plots.
So enter it empty, there's nothing to embolden,
Your chatter is worthless and your silence is golden.

ALI BADSHAH

STAR LIGHT STAR SIGHT

You look up and all you see are stars.

The stars look up and all they see is you.

GIFTED IS YOUR VESSEL

The vacuum is filled after purging through the
   night.
Gifted is your vessel, topped up with new light.
Your animal turns, unwilling to fight.
The silence is deafening.
The noise is bright white.
The plight that turned to blight departed on the last
   flight.
New flames reach up to limitless height.
Now you're left in the centre, learning how to live
   right.

INTERSPACE

I live between the orchestra of energy
  That forms this body and mind.

The interspace that neither can perceive is me.

Light and dark, all at once.

Living in and around the fraction of matter
  That my mind thinks matters.

I am free.

SCALE

There are an infinite number of black holes, nebulas, and galaxies spinning inside of us at any given moment.

HEALING MAGICIAN

When the mind seems over it,
But the body still remembers,
Soaking your coat like rainy Novembers,
Light up a fire in the pit of your heart,
So that embers can dry you and heat a new start.

Memories of the flesh never truly die,
They live in our silos reaching up to the sky,
We try to forget but get caught in our eye,
Tears and the fears have us living a lie.

Our only permission is to change our condition,
Truth is the body's healing magician.

ALI BADSHAH

LIGHTEN UP

Be the light of you.

LEAVE YOURSELF

The time it takes to identify with yourself pulls you out of the moment.

So, the only way to be truly present is to leave yourself out of it.

ALL IN

The heavens and hells,
Past, present, and future,
Everyone and no one,
Nothing and everything,
Have only ever and always will,
Live and die within you.

ALI BADSHAH

YOUNG & TIMELESS

The rebel keeps you young.

The mystic keeps you timeless.

THE ASHES OF YOU

The fires recede,
The ashes of you,
Smoulder and bleed,
To form someone new,
Fresh pain for fresh starts,
Rain refreshes our hearts,
And washes us in the True.

POWER YOU

We
Live
Through
Storms
And
Learn
How
To
Be
Them

BABY FACE

Rocking and cradling your infant self,
Looking down at your own delicate face,
You see the love and focus,
The joy and certainty,
Beaming from every chub and fold,
And you make a promise to your baby,
That you will remember who they are,
Who they came as,
And who they came to be,
That all the time spent in the dark,
Has made you fall back in love with the light,
Has made you fall back in love with you.

ALI BADSHAH

GRATEFUL

When the flesh in your chest is ground up and
  pressed,
All you can do is be grateful.

When the cracks in your mind have you stuck in
  rewind,
All you can do is be grateful.

When the bonds that you held are cut and expelled,
All you can do is be grateful.

And when you breathe heavy sighs with tears in
  your eyes,
All you can do is be grateful.

COORDINATES

Gratitude
Is
The
Attitude
That
Connects
Your
Longitude
With
Your
Latitude

GAME PLAN

Learn from the whole of your past, be completely involved in your life right now with zero entanglements, and imagine your brightest future.

SERVICE

Be ready to serve what you manifest.

THE HEART OF SUCCESS

The passion you bring to the idea is the heart of its success.

YOU SOURCE

When everyone and everything you love comes to pass, it's an opportunity to realize that they were never the source of your joy or suffering – it's always been, and will, be you.

BUTTERFLIES

Butterflies
Land
On
You
When
They
Feel
The
Light

LOVE MAKER

Make love with your life.

LOVE

GIFT

After the deepest sorrow,
When your face is soaked,
And your heart lets out a bottomless cry,
A joy washes over you,
As your dark and heavy turn to light,
What a gift!

THE PROCESS

Love. Learn. Forgive. Repeat

DISAPPEAR AND BE CLEAR

Some loves seem lost in the fog of fear,
Others feel swayed by what the charlatans hear,
We mourn their death,
We shed a tear,
Take in a deep breath and submit to the Seer,
For love is manifest, ever-present, and near,
The loss is illusion,
Like the life we hold dear,
So let's embrace the real magic,
Love's ship at our pier,
And sail deep in our heart,
To disappear and be clear.

EXQUISITE

Create exquisite sensations.

FREE WINE

You'll always be free,
There's no way to confine.

I'll enhance your experience,
Through the clarity of mine.

And in moments of confusion,
Let our kindness shine.

It's our lifelong joy,
To stay true and align.

Doing it together requires
Crushing the vine.

So let's love the unknown,
And drink our well-earned wine.

RAVISHING THE GODDESS

The outcome is me ravishing you,
And then taking you up to the goddesses,
Every night.

The purpose is to express my gratitude,
And to be love in action.

RISE & SHINE

We're not just falling in love with each other.

We're being love and rising in it, shining in it, together.

NEVER SEPARATED & ALWAYS TOGETHER

The connective love energy in and between us is boundless. It's beyond time and space.

When you feel your heartstrings being pulled by thoughts of loved ones, deceased or those living afar, rest assured that they're feeling it too.

We're never separated and always together.

LOVING IN THE MORTAL REALM

Love without entanglements,
And lust without possession,
Must be the goals of the earthly one,
Whose end game is ascension.

DARK LOVE

The creatures in the dark decay are worthy of love.

THE ALL-FORGIVER

We bear maulings from monsters,
Who hide in plain sight,
Our hearts bleed for their souls,
As they kill their own light.

The pure All-Forgiver gives us His might,
To help us move on,
To help make our lives right.

So we forgive and we love,
Then fly away like the dove,
As the monsters die slow in the night.

ALI BADSHAH

THE MOTHER'S LOVE

Everyone can be reborn in the love that our minds and bodies can't comprehend.

Thank you, Madré.

GHOSTWRITER

Let your love story write itself.

ANGELS & BEASTS

Reflecting back to us,
Both angel and beast,
The loves of our life,
Lead to famine or feast,

Some point out our strengths,
While others show us as weak,
Still more do the most,
And even more do the least,

The path to our peak,
Be it north, south, or east,
West is best travelled,
When what we seek is deceased.

SUN LOVE

Love is giving all of you unconditionally with no prospect of return.

It's being the Sun, shining down on all and giving life without question.

INNER PRISM

Falling off the edge of Ego's schism,
Brings us back in step with Life's sweet rhythm,
Our light bends and dances through the inner
  prism,
Of reflection and surrender,
The heart of mysticism.

THE HEART THAT CANNOT CLOSE

When life cracks your sternum,
And pulls apart your cage,
Exposing your beating chest,
You breathe a bit deeper,
And feel everything that passes through,
Both fresh air and debris land,
Without prejudice,
On the heart that cannot close.

ALI BADSHAH

LIFE

DESIGN LIFE

In a realm where we are the creators,
All triumphs and tragedies are of our own design.

THOUGHTFUL HOME

We can place our focus anywhere within our inner cosmos.

The infinite suns, moons, stars, rainfalls, summer nights, and passionate kisses that live in every speck of our being can be our home if we want them to be.

THE CHOSEN FEW

'Family' is a label often used in vain,
First placed on those with same blood and vein,
Obligatory ties through ancestral chain,
The love may be real but forced all the same.

When the accolades pour,
They come out to adore,
But when you suffer in agony,
They lock their front door,
Judging your pain and placing full blame,
It's easier to dismiss you than get caught in the rain.

Real family is open and share the same skies,
They weather the storms and bask in the highs,
Wiping the tears from each other's eyes.

The ones who do are the ones for you,
Families are made by the chosen few.

ALI BADSHAH

MASTERS ARE SLAVES

The difference between the masses and the masters
is that the masters are grateful for being slaves.

CASH OUT

When the teachings of prophets,
Are exploited for profits,
Cash out.

BOUND COLLECTION

Leaping with imagination,
To our final moment,
We can look back on our life's story,
And see how all the scenes connected,
That every chapter was necessary,
For us to complete our journey.

Taking the time to do this often,
Helps us move past the heavier pages,
The crises and climaxes,
And to keep reading,
With love,
Our beautifully bound collection.

PREVENTATIVE MEASURES

Giving attention to our intentions
helps prevent tension.

THE ONLY SOLUTION

In the search of our suffering's conclusion,
The egos driving intellects turn truth into illusion,
When the only solution is love and inclusion.

WE HAVE THE POWER

Our only point of control, and the only thing that matters, is how we feel.

Love, joy, fun, happiness, ease, clarity, courage, freedom, fulfillment, abundance, and their lack, all start and end within us.

We have the power.

MMM

We are the mirrors, muses, and miracles in our lives.

CHIPPING TEETH

Manufacturing shame is a worthless game,
Guilt and blame are much the same,
Crafted by egos not owning the truth,
The youth and the elder both chipping a tooth,
Biting down on themselves to prove that they care,
Instead of loving it all and living aware.

TRUST

Trust that right now is the absolute best.

WE'VE ALWAYS KNOWN EACH OTHER

My teacher's teacher, essentially my grand-teacher – bless his soul – spoke to me only on two occasions. Both at Dergah.

The first time was shortly after I started on this path. My light was dim. My ego's heart was shattered and slowly being pieced back together. He looked at me and said, "You're young." That's it. That's all he said. Years later, the last time I saw him and just before he passed on (at the age of 96), he held my hand in the gentlest way and said, "We've always known each other." It brings me to tears, every time I reflect on that moment and his words.

Nothing is ever truly foreign to us. We're made of the same stardust, and the rivers that flow through me are the ones that flow through you. We see ourselves in each other's eyes and hearts – in our darkness and our light. We've always known each other because, in Truth, there is no other.

Thank you, Cemil Baba.

ZARP

Living in joy while weathering pain is to kiss the swords that pierce you.

TMP TMP TMP TMP

Temptations tempered through the tempo of temples.

OUR GOLDEN GATE

The opener of our golden gate is a key.

Like all keys, it has two parts:
The blade,
Which slides into the keyway of the lock;
And the bow,
Which sticks out,
So that we can apply torque by turning it.

The blade of our key is focus,
It's bow is faith,
And we turn it with the power of gratitude.

ALI BADSHAH

NO COMPETITION

The greatest creator competes with no one.

COSMIC EMBRACE

The ties that bind across time and space,
Help me to feel the essence of your face.
The pace of the race to have you back in place,
Leaves my ego winded and hungry for a taste.
But to chase is to debase the value of our case,
So I trance end my ego and give a cosmic embrace.

HOMEWARD BOUND

Living in line with your vision and purpose is to forever feel at home.

CRYSTAL LIGHT

Crystals with cracks inside,
Shining and waning and wishing to find,
A filler to fill the false feelings of failure,
The cracks in the crystals calling for a saviour,
Dimmed and dumbed by the devious drum,
Of the Cracker with a rhythm cold and numb,
Fearful of both life and death,
It fools crystals into cracking until their last breath,
Illusionary cracks distorting the Light,
Crystals shine bright,
Success in sight.

ALI BADSHAH

ABC

The ABCs of Present Moment Awareness:

Active Alignment
Being Balance
Carefree Certainty

ART

The alchemy of transmuting your presence,
emotions, experience, and imagination into a
creative expression felt outside of you is art.

FOCUS

Stop staring into the storm.

Raise your head and heart to the rainbow all around you.

NO UNCERTAIN TERMS

Power and freedom come from surrender to
uncertainty.

AIRING GRIEVANCES

The Heart and the Ego sat at a table,
To air their respective grievances,
The Ego went on and on,
About anything and everything,
Fearing this, hating that, and wanting more,
While the Heart sat in silence,
Listening to the Ego's never-ending list,
When the Ego paused to take a breath,
The Heart calmly said,
"You will die one day... and I love you."

CATALYST

Eyes open
Heart broken
Fire spoken
Light awoken

MOTION POTION

Passion
Is
The
Potion
That
Puts
Minds
In
Motion

ALI BADSHAH

REALEST ESTATE

The realest estate,
Is our living state,
A villa of love,
Or a hovel of hate,
No mortgage required,
And it's never too late,
To build on our hearts,
A home that is great.

ALI BADSHAH

PERFECT

All the raindrops and rays of sunlight land on their mark.

THE PRICE IS RIGHT

There's no cover charge on spirituality.

It's free admission with full submission.

SINGULARITY

An enlightened life,
Is the joyful journey inward,
Deeper into the Singularity,
At the centre of our dying star.

HELP IT GROW

We place our joy
Outside ourselves
And all we get is pain.
So help it grow
Within your heart
And pay no mind to gain.

ALI BADSHAH

THIRD EYE CRY

As I feel tears of ecstasy,
Flowing from my third eye for the first time,
You show me that there's been far too much doing,
And nowhere near enough being.
Alhamdulillah.

ONE RHYTHM

Our
Hearts
Come
Together
And
Beat
To
The
Same
Rhythm

ALI BADSHAH

TREATY OF SELF

Make peace with the monsters.

THE DAYS I REMEMBER

On the days I remember,
I open my heart and mind,
My intuition and imagination,
With awareness and gratitude,
To pray for you,
For your happiness,
And good fortune,
For your increasing strength,
And the expansion of your heart,
I can do it from anywhere,
From my bed,
My grave,
And across the realms,
On the days I remember.

GROUND RULE

Respect yourself and the rest will follow.

THE TIMES

Remember the times when you felt the light beaming from your face, the certainty radiating from your head to your toes, and the joy vibrating inside every fibre of your being.

AMN

Increase the Light inside of us and outside of us.
Remove the fears and darkness from our hearts.
Remove it from inside of us and outside of us.
Increase the love, courage, health, wealth, subtlety,
  praiseworthiness, and strength inside of us and
  outside of us.
Bring what's best for us into our lives and remove
  what's worse from our lives.
Increase our faith in you.

ABOUT THE AUTHOR

Ali Badshah is an artist, storyteller, rebel, and mystic: A whirling dervish who stars in Oscar® nominated and critically acclaimed films, along with hit television shows and comedy specials streaming all over the world.

Please visit www.ghostflowersbook.com and www.goodbadshah.com for more details.